ROBERT PLANT
lullaby and... THE CEASELESS ROAR

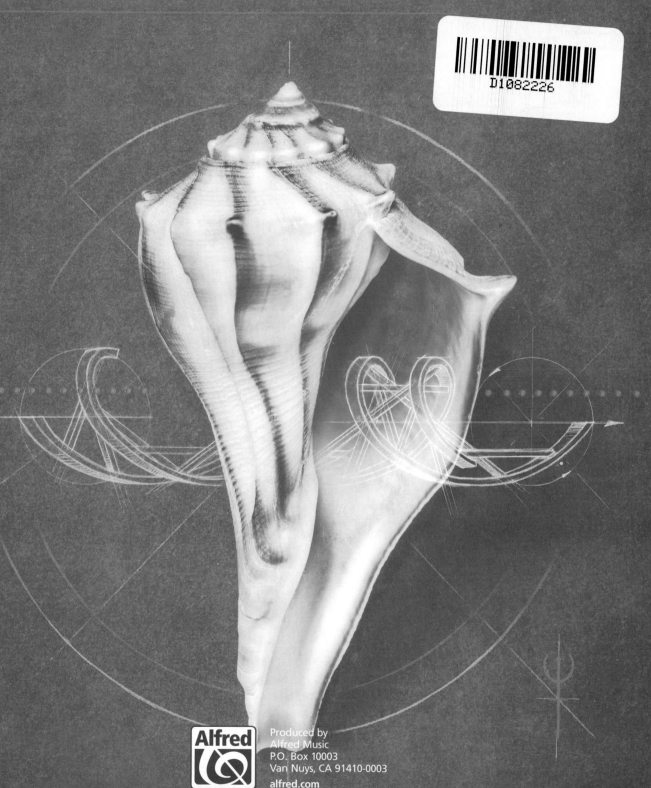

Alfred

Produced by
Alfred Music
P.O. Box 10003
Van Nuys, CA 91410-0003
alfred.com

Printed in USA.

No part of this book shall be reproduced, arranged, adapted, recorded, publicly performed, stored in a retrieval system,
or transmitted by any means without written permission from the publisher. In order to comply with copyright laws, please apply for
such written permission and/or license by contacting the publisher at alfred.com/permissions.

ISBN-10: 1-4706-1980-6
ISBN-13: 978-1-4706-1980-0

Cover Illustrations: Dan Winters
Art Direction: Brett Kilroe and Geoffrey Hanson

 Alfred Cares. Contents printed on environmentally responsible paper.

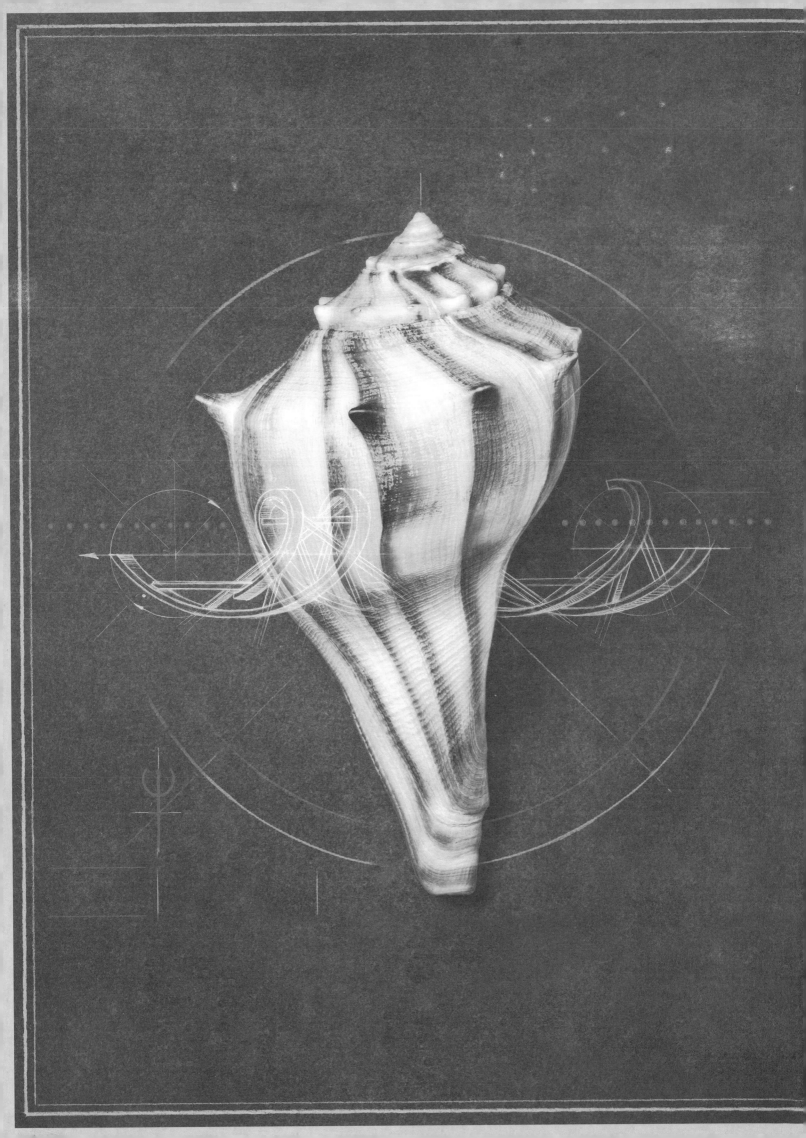

CONTENTS

LITTLE MAGGIE

Words and Music by
ROBERT PLANT, JUSTIN ADAMS,
LIAM TYSON, WILLIAM FULLER,
DAVID SMITH, JOHN BAGGOTT
and JULDEH CAMARA

6-St. Banjo arr. for Guitar, tuned as follows:
⑥ = D ③ = G
⑤ = A ② = A
④ = D ① = E

Moderately ♩ = 124

Intro:

*A

6-St. Banjo *(arr. for gtr.)*

mf

w/thumb & fingers
let ring throughout

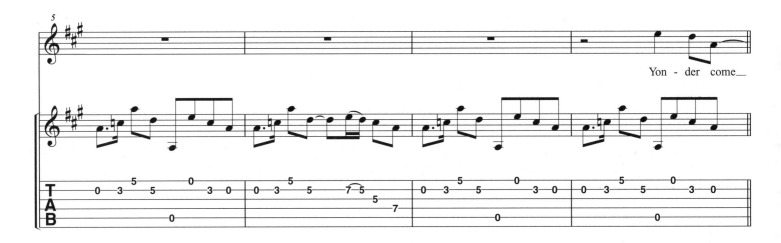

*Chord names are implied throughout.

Verse 1:

Little Maggie - 6 - 1

© 2014 SONS OF EINION PUBLISHING
All Rights Administered by WB MUSIC CORP.
All Rights Reserved

Ritti

6-St. Banjo

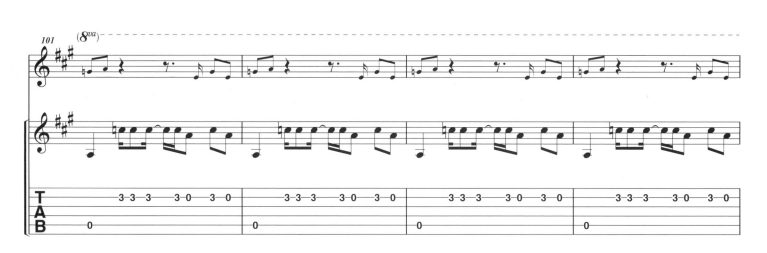

w/Rhy. Fig. 2 *(Elec. Gtr.), simile (see meas. 86-93)*

Ritti tacet

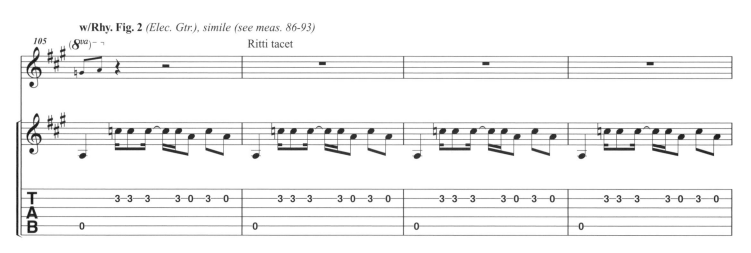

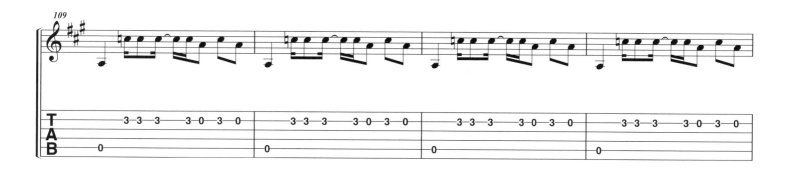

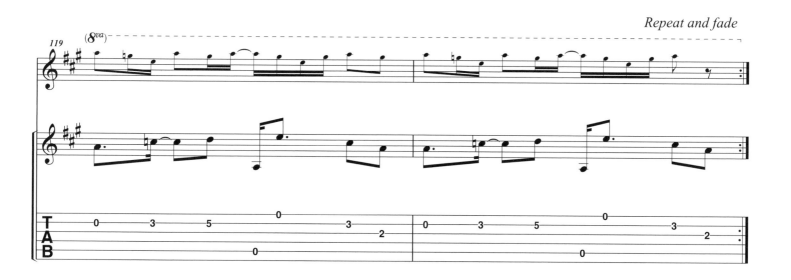

RAINBOW

Words and Music by
ROBERT PLANT, JUSTIN ADAMS,
LIAM TYSON, WILLIAM FULLER
and JOHN BAGGOTT

*Chord frames are for reference throughout.
**Composite arrangement of 2 elec. gtrs.

© 2014 SONS OF EINION PUBLISHING
All Rights Administered by WB MUSIC CORP.
All Rights Reserved

Bridge:

Ⲑ *Coda*

Band re-enters

Elec. Gtr. cont. verse fig, simile

Outro:

POCKETFUL OF GOLDEN

Words and Music by
ROBERT PLANT, JUSTIN ADAMS,
LIAM TYSON, WILLIAM FULLER,
DAVID SMITH, JOHN BAGGOTT
and JULDEH CAMARA

© 2014 SONS OF EINION PUBLISHING
All Rights Administered by WB MUSIC CORP.
All Rights Reserved

*Elec. Gtr. 2 in open G tuning w/capo III (see tuning legend, page 1).
 TAB numbers relative to capo.
**Italicized chord name reflects Elec. Gtr. 2 w/capo III.

Outro:
*G
B♭

Rhy. Fig. 4A
Elec. Gtr. 3 *(clean-tone w/o capo)*

end Rhy. Fig. 4A

mf

Rhy. Fig. 4
Elec. Gtr. 2

end Rhy. Fig. 4

*Italicized chord name reflects Elec. Gtr. 2 w/capo III.

w/Rhy. Figs. 4 *(Elec. Gtr. 2)* **& 4A** *(Elec. Gtr. 3), both 2 times, simile (see meas. 83–86)*
w/Riff A *(Ritti), 2 times, simile (see meas. 5–8)*

Hmm,_____

red hair, rav - en hair, gold like the sun.___

Hmm,_____

all of us in mo - tion, mov - ing on and gone.

Elec. Gtr. 2

Repeat and fade

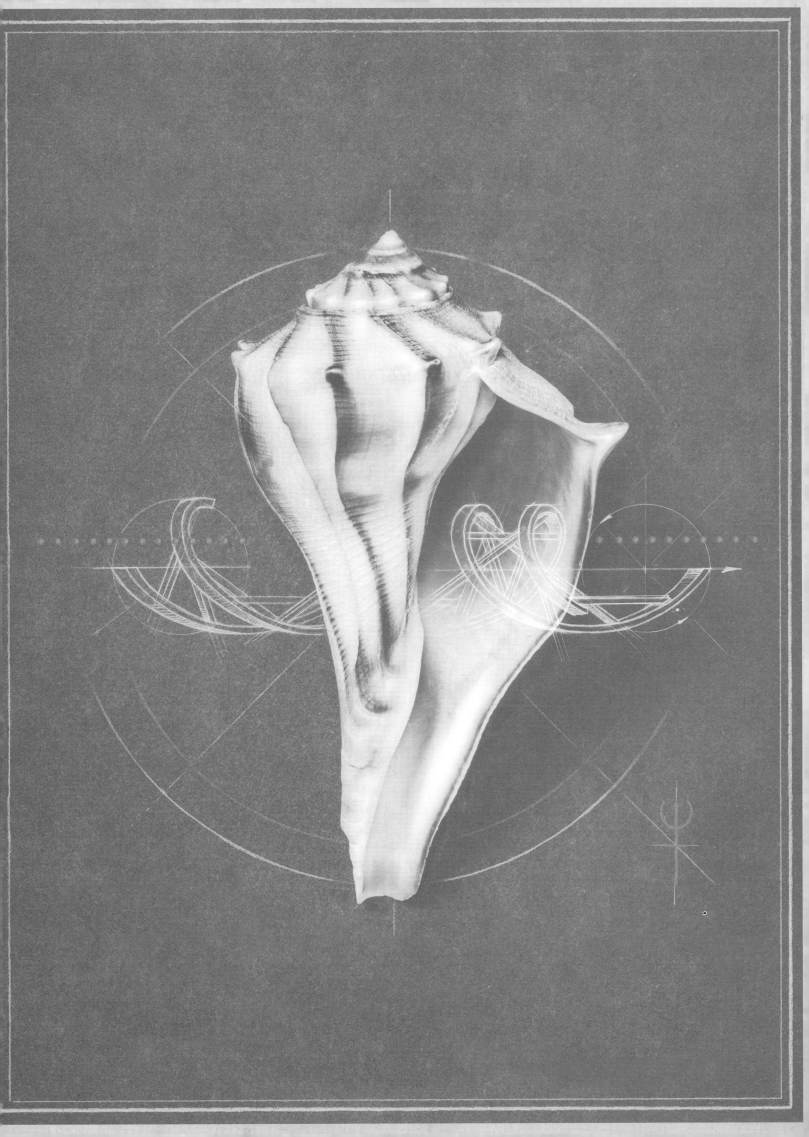

EMBRACE ANOTHER FALL

Words and Music by
ROBERT PLANT, JUSTIN ADAMS,
LIAM TYSON, WILLIAM FULLER,
DAVID SMITH, JOHN BAGGOTT
and JULDEH CAMARA

*Elec. Gtr. 2 enters at meas. 66.
**Chords are implied.

**Percussive hits made by tapping on face of Acous. Gtr.

Embrace Another Fall - 6 - 1

© 2014 SONS OF EINION PUBLISHING
All Rights Administered by WB MUSIC CORP.
All Rights Reserved

Instrumental:

*Elec. Gtr. 1 is a composite arrangement of two Elec. Gtrs.

Verse 5:
Band tacet

*Chords are implied by synth.

Oh,   so blue must turn to grey,___   and out up - on___ the Shire,

all through the frost___ and rain,   I make my home.___

Acous. Gtr. 1

*Verse 6 translation:
 I heard that the Lark
 Has died on the mountain:
 If I knew these words were true
 I would go with a group of men and arms
 To fetch the Lark's body home.

TURN IT UP

Words and Music by
ROBERT PLANT, JUSTIN ADAMS,
LIAM TYSON, JOHN BAGGOTT,
WILLIAM FULLER and DAVID SMITH

*All gtrs. tuned down 1/2 step, w/5th string tuned down 1 1/2 steps:

⑥ = E♭ ③ = G♭
⑤ = G♭ ② = B♭
④ = D♭ ① = E♭

Moderately ♩ = 100

Intro:

G5

*Recording sounds a half step lower than written.
**Elec. Gtr. 1 is a composite arrangement of two Elec. Gtrs.

Verse 1:

w/Rhy. Fig. 1 *(Elec. Gtr. 1) 2 times, simile (see meas. 1–4)*

G5

Char - ley Pat - ton high - way, the mist, the rain, the mud. Some - where east of Tu - ni - ca,___ I'm

close to giv - ing up._____ The car goes 'round in cir - cles, the road re - mains the same. For

help and con - so - la - tion, I'll_____ turn it on a - gain._____ Turn it

Turn It Up - 6 - 1

© 2014 SONS OF EINION PUBLISHING
All Rights Administered by WB MUSIC CORP.
All Rights Reserved

Elec. Gtr. 3 *(w/light dist.)*

Verse 3:

w/Rhy. Fig. 1 *(Elec. Gtr. 1) 2 times, simile (see meas. 1–4)*

G5

lost in - side A - mer - i - ca___ and I'm turn - ing in - side out,___ I'm turn - ing in - to some - one else___ I

heard so much a - bout.___ I'm blind - ed by the ne - on, the right - eous and the might,___ I'm

A STOLEN KISS

Moderately slow ♩ = 78

Words and Music by
ROBERT PLANT, JUSTIN ADAMS,
LIAM TYSON, JOHN BAGGOTT
and WILLIAM FULLER

Intro:
*C
*Suggested chord frames.

Verses 1 & 2:

1. How long has it been like this?
2. How long has it been this way?

Lost and found and lost yet a-gain.
On and on as the days slip a-way. Oh,

Here, in the heat of a sto-len kiss, I make my home.
lost in lan-guage, oh, lost in song, I'm

2.
gone.

Bridge:

I am drawn to the west-ern shore where the light moves bright up-on the

A Stolen Kiss - 3 - 1

© 2014 SONS OF EINION PUBLISHING
All Rights Administered by WB MUSIC CORP.
All Rights Reserved

36

tide. To the lul - la - by _____ and the cease - less roar _____

with a song that nev - er dies. _____

Outro:

Elec. Gtr. 1 *(w/EBow effect)*

Elec. Gtr. 2 *(w/light dist.)*

Elec. Gtr. 1

A Stolen Kiss - 3 - 3

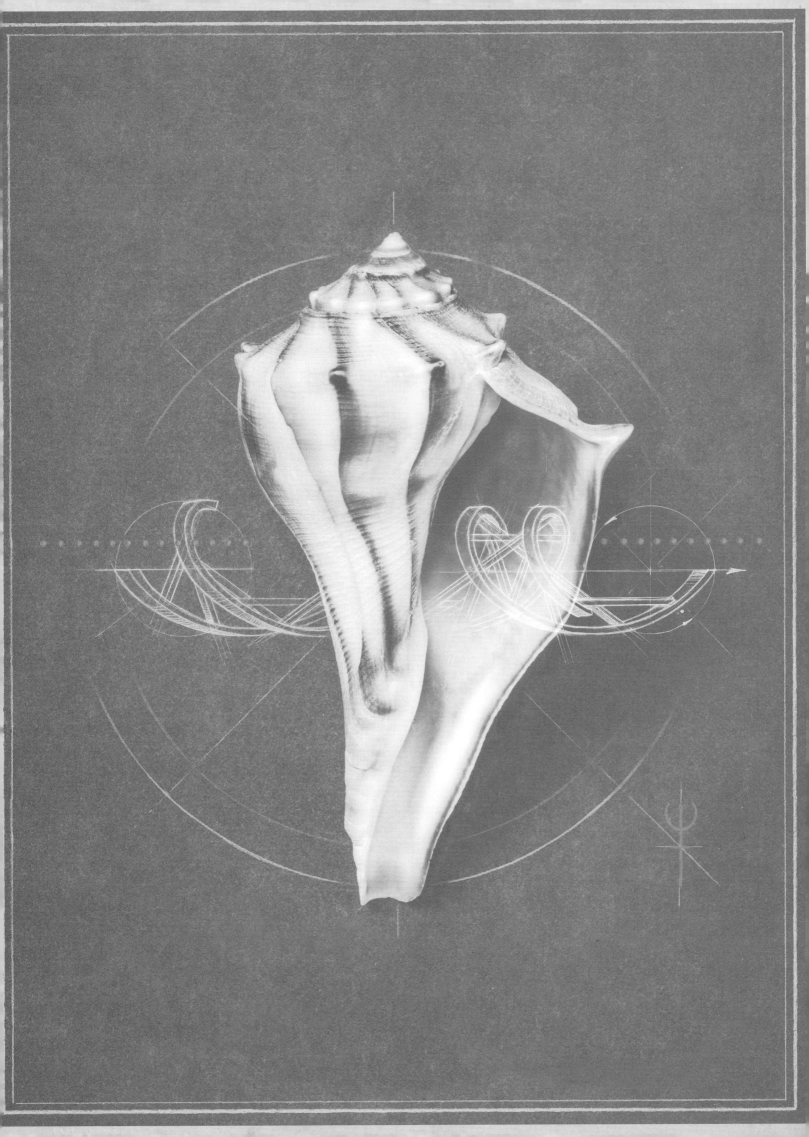

SOMEBODY THERE

Words and Music by
ROBERT PLANT, JUSTIN ADAMS,
LIAM TYSON, JOHN BAGGOTT,
WILLIAM FULLER and DAVID SMITH

Moderately slow ♩ = 88

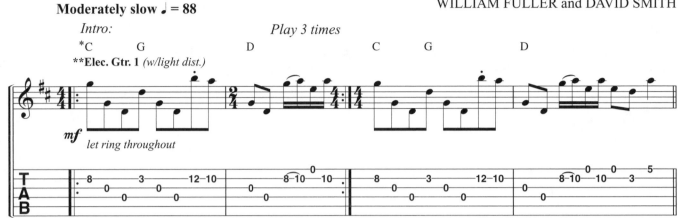

*Chords implied by Bass Gtr.
**Elec. Gtr. 1 is a composite arrangement of 2 Elec. Gtrs.

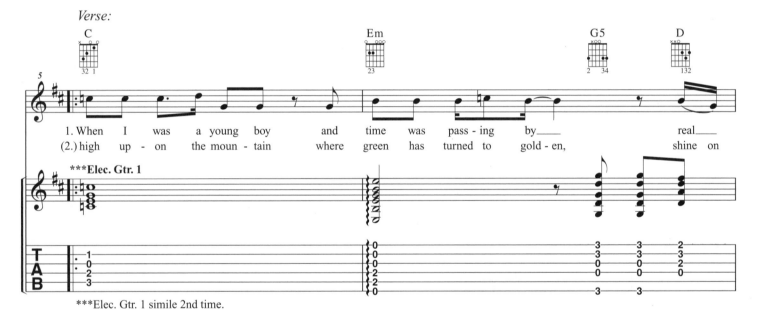

***Elec. Gtr. 1 simile 2nd time.

1. When I was a young boy and time was pass-ing by____ real____ slow.____ And
(2.) high up - on the moun - tain where green has turned to gold - en, shine on so.____ Be -

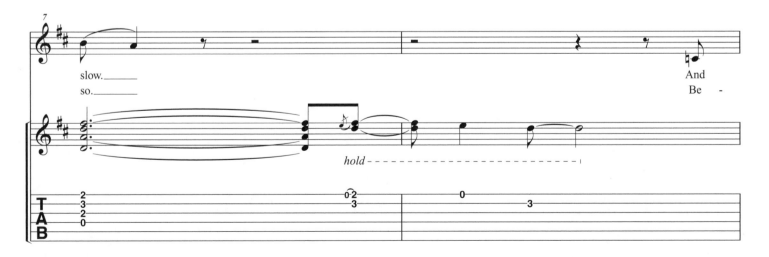

© 2014 SONS OF EINION PUBLISHING
All Rights Administered by WB MUSIC CORP.
All Rights Reserved

*Chords implied by Bass Gtr.

Guitar Solo:

Elec. Gtr. 3 *(w/light dist. & roto-vibe effect)*

Elec. Gtr. 4 *(w/light dist.)*

w/slight P.M. -

POOR HOWARD

(Derivative Work of "PO' HOWARD")

HUDDIE LEDBETTER, JOHN LOMAX, ALAN LOMAX,
New Words by ROBERT PLANT, JUSTIN ADAMS, JOHN BAGGOTT, JULDEH CAMARA,
WILLIAM FULLER and LIAM TYSON

Moderately ♩ = 108

*Chords are implied throughout.

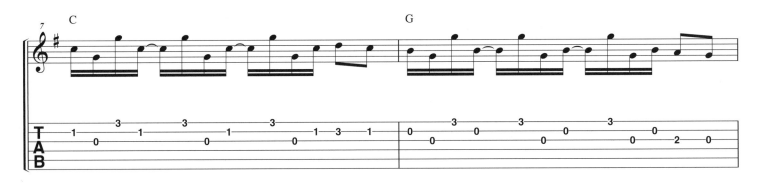

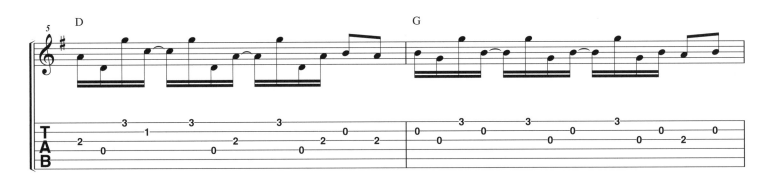

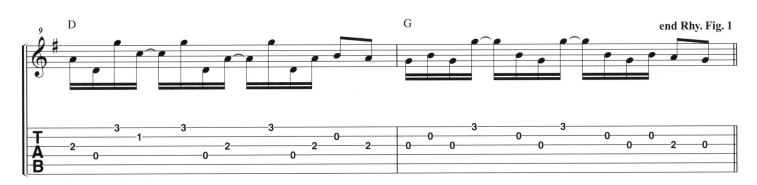

Poor Howard - 5 - 1

© Copyright 1936 (Renewed), 1959 (Renewed), 2014 FOLKWAYS MUSIC PUBLISHERS, INC., New York, GLOBAL JUKEBOX PUBLISHING, Marshall, TX
and SONS OF EINION LTD.
TRO – FOLKWAYS MUSIC PUBLISHERS, INC. Controls All Rights for the World Outside the U.S.A.
All Rights Reserved   Used by Permission

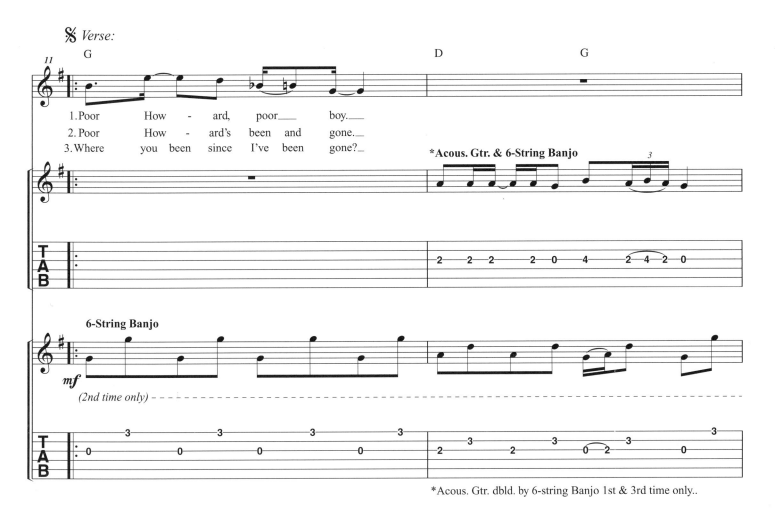

*Acous. Gtr. dbld. by 6-string Banjo 1st & 3rd time only..

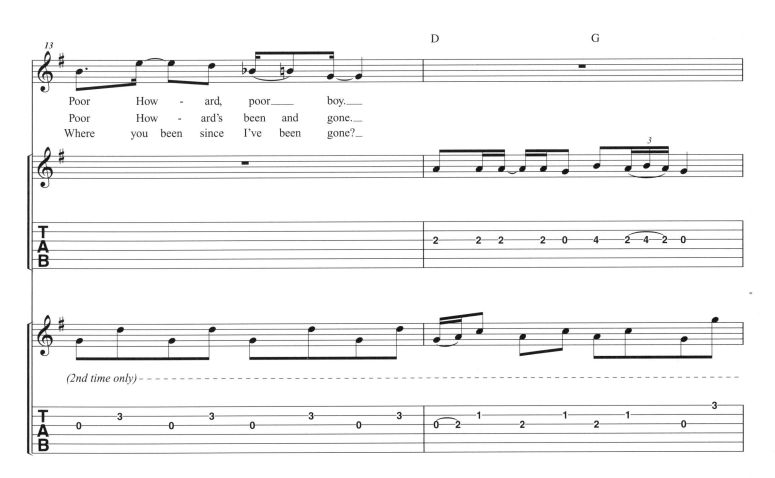

HOUSE OF LOVE

Words and Music by
ROBERT PLANT, JUSTIN ADAMS,
LIAM TYSON, WILLIAM FULLER,
DAVID SMITH and JOHN BAGGOTT

*Chords are implied.

*Bkgd. vocal, 3rd time only.
**Elec. Gtr. 2 simile on repeats.

House of Love - 5 - 1

© 2014 SONS OF EINION PUBLISHING
All Rights Administered by WB MUSIC CORP.
All Rights Reserved

Chorus:

*Elec. Gtr. 2 simile on repeats.

To Coda ⊕

House of Love - 5 - 3

*Elec. Gtr. 3 is played through an octave device,
but arranged here for two guitars.
Up stem notes are played, down stem notes
are the notes sounding one octave lower.

Guitar Solo:

Interlude:
w/Riff A (Elec. Gtr. 1), simile (see meas. 1–8)

D.S. % al Coda
(Go to Verse 3, meas. 17)

Ah._____ Ah._____ Ah._____ Ah._____

Coda

oh, it's the house of love__ burn-ing down._____ Oh._____

Outro:
w/Riff A (Elec. Gtr. 1), simile (see meas. 1–8)

Ah._____ Ah._____

Elec. Gtr. 2

let ring throughout

Repeat and fade

Ah._____ Ah._____

UP ON THE HOLLOW HILL
(Understanding Arthur)

Words and Music by
ROBERT PLANT, JUSTIN ADAMS,
LIAM TYSON, JOHN BAGGOTT
and WILLIAM FULLER

Elec. Gtr. in DADGAD tuning:
⑥ = D ③ = G
⑤ = A ②ַ = A
④ = D ①ַ = D

Freely

* D5

Elec. Gtr. *(w/light dist. & delay)*

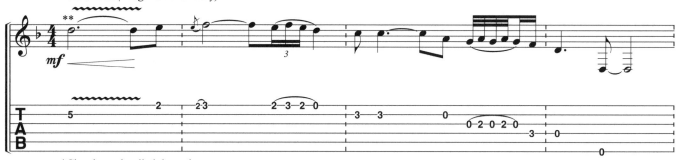

*Chords are implied throughout.
**Volume swell made w/guitar volume knob.

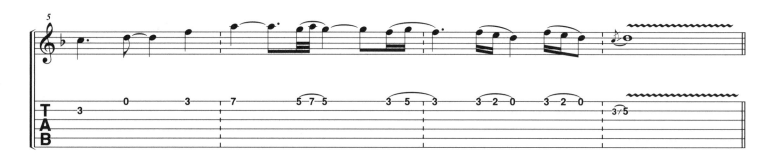

Moderately ♩ = 102

Intro:

Full band enters

D5

let ring throughout

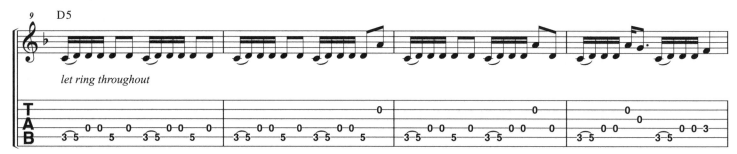

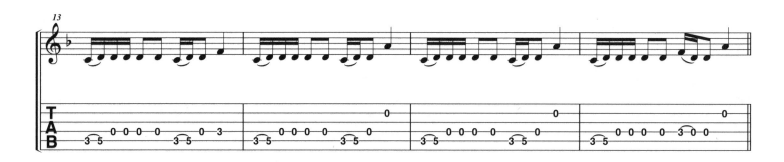

Up on the Hollow Hill (Understanding Arthur) - 6 - 1

© 2014 SONS OF EINION PUBLISHING
All Rights Administered by WB MUSIC CORP.
All Rights Reserved

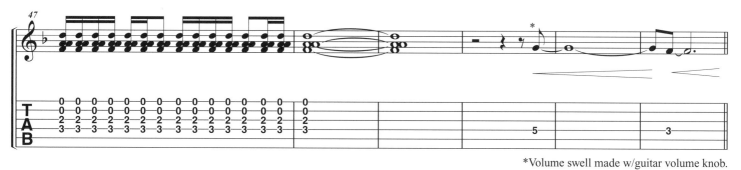

*Volume swell made w/guitar volume knob.

Instrumental:

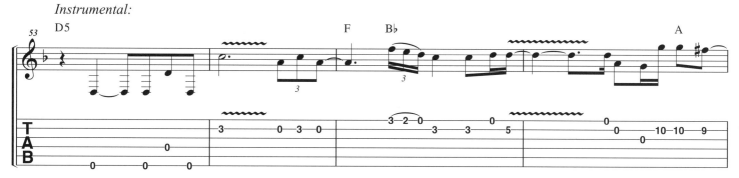

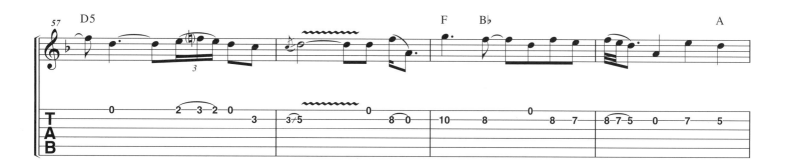

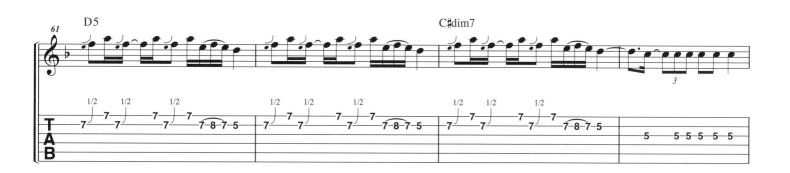

Up on the Hollow Hill (Understanding Arthur) - 6 - 4

58

*Volume swell made w/guitar volume knob.

My..._____

Outro:

My_____ life.

My..._____

ARBADEN
(Maggie's Babby)

Words and Music by
ROBERT PLANT, JUSTIN ADAMS,
LIAM TYSON, WILLIAM FULLER,
DAVID SMITH, JOHN BAGGOTT and JULDEH CAMARA

© 2014 SONS OF EINION PUBLISHING
All Rights Administered by WB MUSIC CORP.
All Rights Reserved

Arbaden (Maggie's Babby) - 4 - 2

den, bad-den___ bad-den ko wel-ly ko dum wel-lan-tam, aaaah.

Begin fade

Repeat and fade

Arbaden (Maggie's Babby) - 4 - 4

GUITAR **TAB** GLOSSARY

TABLATURE EXPLANATION

TAB illustrates the six strings of the guitar.
Notes and chords are indicated by the placement of fret numbers on each string.

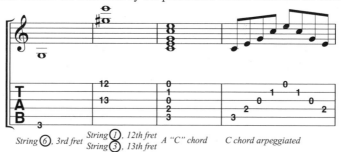

String ⑥, 3rd fret   String ①, 12th fret   A "C" chord   C chord arpeggiated
String ③, 13th fret

BENDING NOTES

Half Step:
Play the note and bend
string one half step
(one fret).

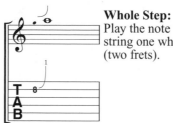

Whole Step:
Play the note and bend
string one whole step
(two frets).

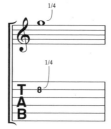

**Slight Bend/
Quarter-Tone Bend:**
Play the note and bend
string sharp.

**Prebend and
Release:**
Play the already-bent
string, then immediately
drop it down to the
fretted note.

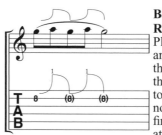

**Bend and
Release:**
Play the note
and bend to
the next pitch,
then release
to the original
note. Only the
first note is
attacked.

PICK DIRECTION

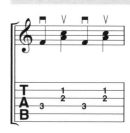

**Downstrokes and
Upstrokes:**
The downstroke is
indicated with this
symbol (⊓) and the
upstroke is indicated
with this (V).

ARTICULATIONS

Hammer On:
Play the lower note,
then "hammer" your
finger to the higher
note. Only the first note
is plucked.

Pull Off:
Play the higher note
with your first finger al-
ready in position on the
lower note. Pull your
finger off the first note
with a strong downward
motion that plucks the
string—sounding the lower note.

Palm Mute:
The notes are muted
(muffled) by placing
the palm of the pick
hand lightly on the
strings, just in front
of the bridge.

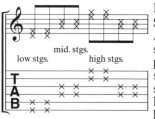

**Muted
Strings:**
A percus-
sive sound is
produced by
striking the
strings while
laying the fret
hand across
them.

Legato Slide:
Play the first
note and,
keeping pres-
sure applied
on the string,
slide up to
the second
note. The
diagonal line shows that it is a slide and
not a hammer-on or a pull-off.

HARMONICS

Natural Harmonic:
A finger of the fret
hand lightly touches the
string at the note indi-
cated in the TAB and is
plucked by the pick pro-
ducing a bell-like sound
called a harmonic.

RHYTHM SLASHES

**Strum
Marks/
Rhythm
Slashes:**
Strum with the indicated rhythm pattern.
Strum marks can be located above the staff
or within the staff.

**Single Notes
with Rhythm
Slashes:**
Sometimes
single notes
are incor-
porated into a strum pattern. The circled
number below is the string and the fret
number is above.

Artificial Harmonic:
Fret the note at the first
TAB number, lightly
touch the string at the
fret indicated in parens
(usually 12 frets higher
than the fretted note),
then pluck the string
with an available finger or your pick.